LAMPLIGHT

Cathy Cain

A Publication of The Poetry Box®

Editing & Book Design by Shawn Aveningo Sanders
Cover Design by Shawn Aveningo Sanders
Cover Image: Glass Art by Cathy Cain
Author Photo by Alex Cain

ISBN: 978-1-956285-74-1
Library of Congress Control Number: 2024915524
Published in the United States of America
Wholesale Distribution by Ingram Group

Published by The Poetry Box®, November 2024
Portland, Oregon
Website: ThePoetryBox.com

for my brave friends who keep their lamps lit long

Someone I loved once gave me
a box full of darkness.

It took me years to understand
that this, too, was a gift.

—Mary Oliver,
"The Uses of Sorrow"

CONTENTS

IN SHADOW

Apache Tear Poem	15
Minutes After	16
The Blue Guitar Advances through Time	17
Orange	18
A Child at Hollywood Park Racetrack	19
Almost Lost	23
Not the Graffiti I Expected	24
Keep Calling	25
Relative	26
The Phone Message	27

MOON MEMORY

With His Kiss	31
Recant	32
Blue Keeps Me Standing	33
Thunder	34
Moon Memory	35
Eye of the Elephant	36
Next Time	37
Mother	38
Cyanotype	39

SHINING FICTIONS

Night Run	43
The Garret	44
Mr. Hedgehog	45
Red Boat	48

She Tells Me about the Mud Flaps 49

It's magic   she says 51

Helianthus Narcissismus 52

She Addresses the River Barge Pilot
Who Passes by Regularly at 3:45 a.m. 53

Shining Fictions 55

Quicksand

Pronouncements at the Supreme Court 59

The Ballot Box 60

Quicksand 61

On the Way to the Piazza del Duomo 62

Manifesto 63

The Children's Corner 64

Lamplight 66

Sunflower Story with Gun 67

Harbored: Lullaby for a Bomber 70

Baskerville 72

Because This Is Home

Animal 75

Why Students Stare Out the Window
—If There Is One 76

House Cleaning 77

A Cordial Welcome 80

Morning 82

Lelooska 83

Laundry 84

Ekphrastic in Anaphora 85

Arches 88

Notes, Inspirations & Citations   91
Acknowledgments & Gratitude   93
Early Praise   95
About the Author   97

IN SHADOW

Apache Tear Poem

My grandfather showed me pieces of black
obsidian, with jagged edges that could slice,
he said, sharper than shards of clear glass.

He polished them long through time,
placed them in my palm so I could
carry them like weighted clouds.

Tumble trouble. Turn it over and over.
Turn the tears once more. Craft the dark,
wear down in poem the pointed pain.

These small stones now smooth in my hand,
sorrow soothed some in my heart.
He said, hold one to your lamp,

see how our night
holds distant light.

Minutes After

Time holds still like this silent bus driver
who sits turning the wheel clockwise
then counter as we speed down the freeway

He keeps the bus steady   as if we existed in just one place
The windshield wipers thup   thup   thup
tick off minutes   hours   in counterpoint
to the round rim of the wheel's slow gathering

Abruptly   to avoid a crash   his hand hits hard on the horn
and we're swirled into shock with sound
a deep bass announcement that blasts time backward
and unsettles   unwinds our internal gyre

Minutes after   the driver reaches up without haste
touches his brow   as we sit quietly remaking our souls
wondering if after all   it's God our bodies hold

THE BLUE GUITAR ADVANCES THROUGH TIME
an Ode to David Hockney

And then, there's Hockney, who strums Stevens' song on Picasso's guitar as he tastes the bittersweet of what it is to be.

Tick It, Tock It, Turn It True.

He honors the many ways things are, paints the world both as it is and the world anew.

On paper or canvas, Hockney's *Invented Man* horses about, edgy and askew, on a stage where romance pings far and echoes. Hockney adds drapes, rendered softly like a shawl, to frame his dry, bright wit in scenes set in sly light and shadow.

The opened curtains, like parting clouds, reveal a rainbow path to the artist's ideals: both the color pop of full-spectrum Real and his Dream-work with cockeyed perspective and hue. Picture planes read flat, yet chairs and vases of flowers seem to advance, full of themselves, like this invented man,

Hockney, who riffs off Picasso's chiaroscuro, changing his touch to pick our many tunes. He plays himself lightly, *the old fantouche*, with whimsy and bravado. Broken apart, he reassembles himself and asserts: When I strut like the Sun, I shall wear a plaid shirt!

But what of our days under overcast clouds, somber resonances, and our thirst to comprehend the stranger depths heard?

When Hockney paints the shadow of the ubiquitous guitar, his mother's dress, his lover's robe, or his cool swimming pool, he teases us, splashes their sparkling songs with quenching savage blues.

ORANGE

I know Atlantis sank

I sank it

it lies there in shadow
deep in memory's thick ocean

green seas swoosh to one side
then the other   cover it completely

my water wings fit just right
tight orange   above my elbows

each day   each night
I paddle non-stop
to stay afloat
above what I know

A Child at Hollywood Park Racetrack

the smell of oil burning   salt   and tar
pumpjacks creaking
big black grasshoppers against the sky

sunshine and stucco   white   and pink
lots of pink   do you like pink?   what are the odds?

at the corner of Larch and East Arbor Vitae
men step off the bus
in a silent line
that heads east to the Track
then disappears

Do not talk to strangers

in the pink stucco house
thin women hold cigarettes
women lost in home perms and hair coloring kits
women working through the odds

Roll up your windows
Lock your doors here
No walking through the alleys

but it's ok to let a child play
alone in an empty dusty lot
even though two doors down
on the other side of the cinderblock wall
a witch stands on her porch

and two blocks past Myrtle
another witch hides in her tropical jungle
between Flower and Osage
its green held in check by the back edge
of the parking lot for the hospital called Centinela

[. . .]

if you look west   along La Brea
Arthur Murray Dance blinks neon
as if you could dance with the bright letters
pull them with you all the way to Hawthorne

and farther   *Randy's Donuts*
at La Cienega and West Manchester
that giant donut hanging out there in the sky
as if you could reach it   pull it to you

and then the Pacific flaring   mimicking
fire on water

to the south   the Drive-In on Century
or maybe Imperial
Pillow Talk   The Solid Gold Cadillac
Alice in Wonderland   Peter Pan
the black speaker box on a post
rays of light swimming through the dark

and right here   edged by South Prairie Ave
is the Kelso School yard
asphalt and dirt
a few dry weeds and torn papers caught
where a child's fingers grip the chain-link fence

she's facing east
but sees in the periphery to her distant left
the pie-wedge of cemetery where
white headstones like small paper boats
are scattered on brilliant green

then she looks directly ahead
across the street   to the racetrack
where men and women stand in lines
like ants to cotton candy
where horses startle and whinny
neigh for food   neigh to run   surrounded
by a sea of cars
bleached and shimmering in the vast lot

:::

and there I am   that child
now in the racetrack lot   in the glare
startled   surrounded
because the carnival has come
with its tents and flags in garish color

I look down   into a metal tub
at a whirling of pale pink wisps

do you like pink?

how large the cloud I am offered
how sweet as it dissolves in my mouth
how raspberry-red the wet remains
left on the narrow white paper cone
a revolting sticky mess
on my hands   my face

under one stall awning   dangle tiny blown-glass horses
and ballerinas   for sale   glinting white fire
if only I could touch them   pull them to me

a man's hand and hairy forearm reach towards them
I back away

a jet screeches so close overhead
as if I could reach up   pull its ample belly to me

more tents and stalls   like small dark cages
windowed stages
here   Big Woman sways
a huge snake draped over her bare shoulders
her ample cleavage

three tents down   her miniature girlfriend sits very still
so alone on a large yellow chair

[. . .]

next   the carrot-haired man flexes his muscles
his entire body tattooed purple blue and flame-orange red

the acrid smell of tar   the smell of the sea
sea of cars glinting   music of salt and tar
of parked car after parked car   the glare
the line of men moving
with white tickets in their hands

what are the odds?

horses whinny in their stalls
switch their tails back and forth
tensed to run
to fly like fire on water

in his tent   a man with no arms or legs
stares back at me   silent on his stage

these cages   these stalls
these gawking grown-ups
this line of men moving

my fingers grip the chain-link fence

the sky screaming   broken
busted through from the descent into LAX
so close   as if I could reach up   fix it

forget the odds

Almost Lost

It was not when she said that she didn't feel well
nor when I turned and saw her in the backseat
her lovely leaf-yellow face gone ashen

and not when I pulled her out
from the bathroom stall by her feet
where she'd gone limp
sunk off the stool   unconscious

nor when I laid her on her back
on the hard cold floor
and placed my ear near her lips

but when I stood up   looking down at her
before the medics burst through the door
when for an instant   I forgot the panic   the sirens

even that she was my friend
and I remembered a photograph I once saw
of flowers in a vase in afternoon light   past their peak
with one petal fallen

Like a dream almost lost
her strong slight body bent at odd angles
a failing stem with twisted leaves   folded like origami

She looked like a geisha loosened
her long black hair swirling around her torso
her silk kimono embroidered
with lavender on yellow   edged in red

her cheeks and brow white   as if powdered
a touch of rouge on her lips
fading   contorted   a petal
paper-thin

Not the Graffiti I Expected

The two of them, sulky,
walked among the tables and chairs—
ducked into the restroom just off my classroom.
Her friend returned. I waited.
A sense she'd been gone too long—
I glanced at her empty chair, saw the X-Acto knife
on the table, still there.

Nonchalantly, I edged towards the bathroom.
A sense she'd been gone too long—
I opened the door.
She sat on the tile floor
in front of the full-length mirror,
mascara stains streaking her face,
her bare arms marked

with fine red lines—
straight, deliberate.
Not the graffiti I expected.
She looked up, into the mirror,
at herself and me behind her—
and with a sardonic smile, said,
This time, instead, I chose permanent ink.

In the mirror, her sardonic smile,
mascara stains streaking her face.
Her bare arms marked
with fine red lines—
straight, deliberate.
She'd been gone too long.
I opened the door.

Keep Calling

She walks the railroad tracks,
learning their rhythm,
rubbing her bare bones from within,
her coat of many colors slipping off,
exposing her soft shoulder of shame.

Gingerly she foots each tie between
gleaming rails. Train whistle's red refrain.
Hidden on either side by dark trees,
she would not be quickly discovered.

Who said she would
respond to her called name?
Eyes closed, first one foot then the other,
she walks the long corridor ahead,
unwinds a thread of words unsaid.

RELATIVE

That house on my back,
house of memories.

Fireflies and soaking heat,
the smell of mothballs.

Almost always addled, she
misplaced the nine different calendars

on which she had written
the now forgotten.

Did she eat the cat medicine?

Shame up against the back wall
flailing a switch—

twig and branch shadows
on her face, her arms, her wrists.

She set the roof on fire,
and the family knew it.

Even so, they sat there
playing scrabble.

Egg sac, embryo of madness,
like the pupil of her eye,

looking off to the side.
Before the consonants,

the first primal vowel.
The clawing howl.

Fire's craven scent.

THE PHONE MESSAGE

well this is N
so so one
I just wanted to say
how are you? both of you?
I could
I'd like to talk I'd like to talk
to hear you again
I've got this
I cannot see everything
cannot say everything now

this is N at
I live with
the daughter now
own my own
and so he's trying to call me
she's for you
I'm in I'm in
let's see if I can say
I wish I can say it
maybe you can get it from a gal
the galleys
and he can find out about you
about me
we'll try I'll try
to hear it   the words
because I've had a
you know
and cannot   can't say everything
but I'll try to
both of you soon. Ok?
I'll keep trying
call me OK?
thank you

this is N at Normandy
I cannot see everything
cannot say everything now
but I can tell
tell a little bit
that you're
that I'd like to hear from you
call me OK?

MOON MEMORY

WITH HIS KISS

each winter together
her husband gave her with his kiss
the gift of a Nutcracker

later   her gift tucked
back in its box for safe keeping
her husband ill   she heard

Am I dying?

Asleep   he put on his red coat
sturdy pants and shiny black boots
even a blazing gold-fringed cape   ready now

his cheekbones and arms carved thin
the hinge of his jaw dropped
his belly   soft baby skin there
his bed   like a box   like a coffin   like a cradle

RECANT

A talker   jovial   vital
a builder of canoes
a paddler in clear river water

That summer day   there were
deep reflections at each bend,
until one swift stroke
then dark watery turbulence
with no escape

It was left to the youngest son
to decide to save him
all but his ability
to speak and write
to manage decently
his thought   now silenced
by his own garble

It was left to the eldest son
to find him dead from a bullet
explanation gone
all but his final gesture
a cascade of rapids over rock
a whitewater crash
an avalanche of intent

BLUE KEEPS ME STANDING

a Synesthesia

Every Dish a Taste Distinct   flashes in neon on the Chinese restaurant sign behind the neurologist who stands at the window   I ask him   a spot?   *yes   a spot*   turquoise pulses through me   I am fright   I am electric blue   he says   *a change in tone*   sapphire shields me against the onslaught   *spasticity   a function of speed*   lapis consumes me   *as opposed to   rigidity*   navy stays me   *not a stroke   nor a tumor*   robin's egg blue   *but an inflammation*   my breath royal blue   I ask   an inflammation?   *yes   a spot*   I say   so a spot   a cobalt spot   how can this be?   Egyptian blue engulfs   there are larkspur bruises on my son's tender skin   rush of Prussian blue   cyan   aquamarine   I've come undone   I plead to the God of Distinctions   a steel-blue prayer

THUNDER

You ask the nurse
what time
will the doctor come round
with answers
The nurse says
He will come
So you wait for the answers
he will not have

The night light is nice
So is the peppermint pink ice cream
with bits of mint green candy

You try not to look
into those windows across
the small stone courtyard
but there   in their faded hospital gowns
are men and women
tubed and wired
and under the fluorescent light
their blue faces
shine so sweetly

You listen to
dream shadows
underwater sounds
high bleep   low buzz
pulsing flow line
of life alive

You listen for the gurney
being wheeled down the hospital halls
coming for you   You listen
for that large rolling sound

Moon Memory

in the dark of the night
the full moon remembers
the absent sun
and reflects back
as we see again
those who are no longer
living their days in the light

Eye of the Elephant

Did you look into the eye of the elephant
past the long lashes
and through the years
of her enormous growth
into the dark pool
the telling of who you are?

Did you look until
you twice tapped
your heavy leg
then lumbered through the gate
and over the fallen acacia tree
to wrap your trunk
around your sister's bones
and carry them to safe ground?

Next Time

When the morning knock came, I expected not a crowd,
but the next-shift hospice nurse.
Mint toothpaste still on my tongue, I rushed through
my mother's darkened room into the entry,
and unthinking, left her bedroom door gaping open.
I threw wide the heavy front door,
my hand on the brass doorknob, sweet air rushing in.
There, on the porch, the nurse, and the rare winter sun.

Mother, in her bed, working hard to depart in seclusion,
lay exposed. She bolted from morphine's half-sleep to sitting,
cried out through her glazed blue eyes, "No!"

Next time, I would not intrude on her dream-leaving labor.
Next time, surely, I would respect her solitude,
    pause, and close her door.
And yet I craved more light, more blinding light.

MOTHER

Often   when I played in the low surf
she would relax nearby on the beach
sitting at the edge of the water
Now   all I have left of her
sits high in a small pot
near the edge of my closet shelf
the rest of her   scattered in the sea

When I hold the pot
its roundness in my palm
and dip my finger in
to place a faint print   of her
on my wrist   the ash
resists the shift
over the edge that divides us
as if she were still   protecting me

CYANOTYPE

Jackson a big boy
Jackson solid like a car   tumbling
cartwheeling through his life
Jackson gone

The cyanotype prints of delicate peonies
his artist mother keeps making
ghost flowers of intricate blues
cloudy blues

blues transparent like rain
absolutely perishable   ghosts
she shapes from light

ghost flowers she lays like a blanket
ever so lightly   over him
flower after flower

SHINING FICTIONS

Night Run

-after La Bohème, *Santa Fe Opera*

After the opera, the singer stepped off the stage, away from his last exhilaration, and travelled back into his own wide landscape.

His eyes followed along the far stony mountain rim surrounding his thought. Could he move into this late sunset of stillness, this bronzed zone, without her? Could he remember the shape of breath in her rib cage, the rise and fall of her sternum?

In his mind, he pressed his lips once more to her thin wrist, tasted her scent that dropped him, lost. Around him, he saw fragile flowers tethering down a hushed lullaby, the blue coming of night. He thought of her breath disappearing into the desert, put his ear to the ground, and heard her voice like a pomegranate of ruby desire.

Under the slurry of stars, he ran. Panting, freighted with the weight of searching, he felt a keen leaning into some other sector of mind, one of stones with secrets, their own, not his. Each dark rock made an exclamation point in the language of sand. Cactus silhouettes stood like petroglyphs, forgotten runes. Stones, and stones.

Above the dark rim of valley floor, the crescent moon rose like the curved edge of her hand gently rocking his dream land, keeping his hard secrets like stars, alive, safe in their habitat of empty space. Even the lovely gesture of her death.

In the lush night, running to stay there. Running to be with her. His wild, white shape caught like a cactus bloom in faint moonlight.

THE GARRET

~after *La Bohème,* The Santa Fe Opera

The walls of the garret   like stanzas   angle out
for the lovers   and passion stages a grand release
into the wealth of their bodies   Their shining hearts
their bold exchange of energy like a box of polished rocks

So easy to enter this plush extravagance
this happy algorithm of jeweled permanence in the mind

yet too soon comes the travesty of poverty
the boney puny nothingness
the grayed nubbins of worn boards   and rotting garbage
the world of those who've been sacked   sucked dry
left raw by disease   and private wars gone public

Too soon the lovers will eat winter's paucity
the writer burn his words to stave off cold
cruel illness force their sweet talk to slide
into restless curses   as love shatters like stone
when his jasper mind and her tiger's eye collide

Mr. Hedgehog

Poor Mr. Hedgehog,
you want to find a wife,
but your way
is the only way.
What a life.

Nocturnal, you sit
rolled tight,
eyes closed
to the light
of everyday stuff.

An adorable hypocrite—
too bad you're rough,
so far, avoiding the bite
of this vixen, this sassy viper.
With professorial power,

you're a prickly predator.
You bristle each spine,
an abstract line—
Marxism, meliorism,
functionalism, interpretivism.

But these abstractions hide
your heart, a complex prism,
that vulnerable story
you're too proud to recount.
Her story, somehow,

you can't figure out.
She knows
(you're missing the point)
that the interpretation
of the state of the nation

[. . .]

should be joint.
Her sapphire scales,
her emerald eyes,
her ruby tongue,
this particular snake,

could make you ache.
You sense she's a sage.
Still, you won't engage.
Rather than trust her hunch,
you'd prefer her for lunch.

Cute as you are,
you've always assumed
any juicy female
come your way
would swoon

to have you as a groom.
You do not equate
her sparkling silence
with jeweled defiance
that will not abate.

You protect yourself,
dismiss her as dense.
You can't seem to translate
her sinuous views.
Is she too much for you?

Your narrow life so chilling,
what female would be willing
to entertain matrimony
with your spiny
male hegemony?

Just watch her now,
as she slithers from the tussle,
and leaves you troubled, puzzled,
more than slightly ruffled.
You're lucky she didn't nip your muzzle.

Poor Mr. Hedgehog,
you want to find a wife,
but if your way
is the only way,
she says,
Not on your life!

RED BOAT

a red boat's reflection
on still water
just broken
the waltz on the surface
of dissonant flashes
his eyelashes
skimming her forehead

his breathtaking deception

She Tells Me about the Mud Flaps

I never learned how to avoid the loneliness
of dog shit on an empty sidewalk
and that line of ragged prayer flags
every time we crossed the bridge

He smelled sour when he came home
from a long day unloading boxcars
He too   loathed the odor of railroad
grease and rotten potatoes

He came home smiling
with a clenched jaw
and looked elsewhere
when I greeted him

This was a love like driving a Ferrari
with the emergency brake locked on
like a tree root straining
to break through cold concrete

like a sloth slogging through a labyrinth
a gaggle of gaily colored balloons caught
high in winter branches   a dish aimed
at the sky   listening for a reply

The fire hydrant of delight shut off
Rats in the sewer
Elsewhere   anywhere but here
was where he wanted to be

I came home from yoga
but forgot my yoga mat
the *oms* there   off key
My own key   fumbling in the door

[. . .]

The kitchen was a mess
My hope for us like the chicken carcass
left out on the counter
I cleared some space

made peanut butter cookies   timed them
to still be warm   but knew he'd come home late
I packed the brown sugar down hard
with my knuckles

That night   downshifting
on the long hill into town   I searched for him
The blank buildings threw no shadow
gave no clue to what I already knew

The streets were a garbled order
Iowa to Carolina   Idaho to Vermont
then Florida   Texas and California
my map of him askew

I parked on a speed bump
across from his rig   its mud flaps
caked and dragging   He was gone
moving on

this charismatic man I loved
like a bad habit
I hit the raw wall between us
my ribs cracking

It's magic   she says

how I think of a friend
and then   that friend calls
how I dream of a volcano
then read of a new eruption

how I drive around to revisit the light
reflecting off a window   and realize halfway
that the light will be altered by the time I return
and it is

how I float on my raft in the sun   my skin
covered with goose bumps from the cold lake
how I realize he will leave
and he does

HELIANTHUS NARCISSISMUS

Sunflower?   she said   *I'm not feeling it*
not in the dead of winter

Outside their window
the cheery sunflower seeds
went round and round

So much remarkable beauty in nature's design
but really   for them   so little intertwining
The Fibonacci whorls of sunflower delight
charming   yet hammered in
a compact pattern that did not open

His part   a sturdy stem   at first glance
steady   with bantering leaves and clever
enticements   his intelligence   his ambition
and all those seeds   housing his secret needs
his beautiful visions   his shining fictions

Her part   the translucent yellow petals
how they lay ruffled   pushed apart from the center
without connection
a soft frame   a sidekick
dismissed   disregarded

The petals' slow bruising through the hot summers
blackened like a dark day   like a screech of rubber
Round and round   the swirl of their shared hours
like good water lost down a drain
a straight-jacketed flower   flawed

Forgiving   still in love   she watched for so long
his smile   his grand gestures   and yes
his stooped shoulders bent with unknown burden

She said   *I watched the flower of us   my shining fiction*
resolutely face each morning sun

She Addresses the River Barge Pilot Who Passes by Regularly at 3:45 a.m.

Down the hill and steep bank of night,
I see only you, your head in silhouette
framed in that small cabin window,
a square illumined
by your ship's one interior light,
your riverboat gliding slowly
on black shine against blacker land.

My child sleeps. I am alone
and frightened in this new house at the forest fringe,
a respite from the storm of a torn marriage,
a wreckage of small quiet deaths.
I've also turned on just one lamp so as not to fall.
I, too, negotiate an opaque swirl, but wonder
if I can navigate what comes next.

I startle at each creak, pace my deck, grab the wheel,
steer my thought, peer into the depth
of what I do not know, take soundings.
Each night, the long waiting
until your brief passing signals
that I'm through the worst hours
of my shape-shifting trouble.

I shall be glad when the morning light arrives
and color is mended, when I can clearly see
the butter-yellow walls in this kitchen nook,
the blue and white pottery on the shelf
above the bay window, and can look out to Douglas Fir,
cloud-frothed skies, and the river below
turned silver.

[. . .]

Dear Bargeman, do you ever glance up
to my one lit window against all that black,
ever take some of the same comfort you've given me?
Thank you for guiding
my weight of fear down the river,
night after night,
floating it into the bright morning.

SHINING FICTIONS

Her first love said
maybe I'll see you again
before the angels come to take me away
and they hugged
and then it was done
and that was their quiet ending

QUICKSAND

Pronouncements at the Supreme Court

On the broad white steps of the Court's portico
among imposing Corinthian columns
we wait in clusters to hear the judges' lofty words
They deliberate rulings regarding our rights
decide how much freedom we each deserve

Yet one day these stately columns may topple
like the present ruins of antiquity   each stone section
become a core sample of momentary reasonings
sliced from the context of history

and today's pronouncements become partially obscured
like rocks at the bottom of a stream   where time
like water   flows over form   rounds out thought
rolls meanings   and once powerful laws
glint only briefly   their colors shifting

The Ballot Box

Even as a child, I knew this was about more than the looming tan canvas booths, with their wood frames and library smell, that had been placed for the day in our emptied dining room.

That evening, neighborhood men and women, just regular folk, sat in the kitchen at our yellow Formica table on which was placed the big box. Grandmother was there too. I listened.

Their voices somber. The slow measured count of each declared ballot number, the repeat call a confirmation of individual choice, unchallenged. The concentration, the careful accounting, the trust that filled our home.

One tic mark for each vote, made by hand on paper, set in groups of five. A diagonal across each vertical four. The pattern that emerged like little gates to freedom.

Quicksand

I awaken to the newspaper's thud on my porch
continued bad news
with its promise of tomahawk
torture and toothless incompetence
a quagmire like Tarzan's quicksand

I don my robe for toast and coffee
avoid the morning mirror
and clear the table
of yesterday's trial and error

Once more I conspire against
the short-sighted causes of Trouble in River City
the claustrophobic carnage described in today's text
Then I dress for treachery and confront
my cowardly complicity in the mirror

On the Way to the Piazza del Duomo

accordion music swelled across the piazza
filled it with love songs   hard to resist   but it was then
just after I passed by two cars parked in the side street
and the pile of filthy rags lying between them
that I sensed moisture   your breath

and I realized that I had seen a forehead   your forehead
your downturned face hidden   cheek propped on the curb
your bruised arm extended on the sidewalk toward me
camouflaged among the foul trash   palm up
your dirty hand with its sores   so repulsive

so vulnerable   so beautiful   you so alive in your grief
like an angel fallen in a heap

blinded   frightened to see my own face
I quickened my pace

Manifesto

the word *manifesto* makes me manic
maddens me with its mythic myopia

manifesto makes me panic
like seeing someone boxed in   trapped
spouting a spiel on repeat   a froth of falsehood

manifesto leads to something clamped down tight

manifesto curls me under the desk
hidden in a dark room
as angry marchers storm
through the halls in a tidal wave
with weighted words on their shoulders
fists in the air
thought narrowed   straight ahead
only to tumble and crash over reason's edge

THE CHILDREN'S CORNER

The teacher's given task year after year
Make them feel safe while they are here.

:::

I'm alert when a small child wraps and rewraps the doll   the paper clip
even a scrap of paper   They tell me her family front door was kicked in

A boy steps off the bus   with his hands held over his shell ears
His eyes cast down   he whispers   *I dream in silence   I live in fear*

A fish market girl sleeps in her clothes and urine
Sequin fish scales shine on her hair   and dirty pale skin

Shredded newspaper he tries to stuff   spills out the grocery bag
Anger strewn wide   Flashbacks   He groans and gags

Ambushed by her parents' friend   hard sex in the shed
Night's acrid odor   Now she sees fire at the edge of her bed

The youngest   amok   jumps ever so slowly from high
As he falls   angel wisps of his fair hair rise

She feels awkward   as her stepfather forces her   as if she could
Her thin arms stretched out   each to balance a telephone book

When she fails   in full-blown rage he holds her head under
the heavy water   his running rant

:::

Half a life later   I lie awake once again watching over them
as they nap   in my hidden corner
They are quiet   curled within

safe for a moment

After each storm
to aid their legal case   I was told not ever to ask
You lovely flower   what happened?   Was it the wind?

LAMPLIGHT

He waits on the deck, cigarette in hand,
a moth among moths of ash flicked around him.
He waits for the sound of her car on the gravel drive,
hovers, grey-shadowed against a story's unfolding,
holding a blanket that soon will engulf her
like an eclipse made by moths as they alight.

He's cut the cords, dumped the phones in the washer.
In the bedroom, he's arranged
a line of her shoes in pairs,
each set like the wings of a moth.
Placed at the center of each pair,
a large kitchen knife.

He steps back inside, closes summer's unlocked door,
listens for her step, nets her with the blanket thrown.
Like a cloud of moths, grey-shadowed and white,
confusion billows, muffles her constricted screams.
His agitated wings flutter to a sharpened focus.
Rape reeks right through her fight.

Rape, not murder, how lucky. But beware,
in unhinged dreams he comes again,
ties her wrists in prayer, forces her under
foul odor, heavy breathing, beating wings.
Moths play a wicked game.
Hide your lamp tonight.

Sunflower Story with Gun

~after David Hockney, *Looking at Pictures on a Screen* (1977) and
Van Gogh Chair (1988)

Scene i

We look through Hockney's eyes at the profile
of a pudgy man in a white suit, his bowtie green,
standing in front of a small print, Van Gogh's
yellow sunflowers, tacked onto a folding screen.

Hockney, seeing things as they are,
accepting, contradicting,
making mysterious space congenial,
a creamy drama. Hockney, the Emperor of Dreams.

Scene ii

Each of Van Gogh's sunflower heads
with Fibonacci's pattern, a galaxy of stars.
Green fire spiraling out, manic, on a stage.
Green madness spilling into night.

Those big heads bopping. Floppy heads,
each with a thousand eyes, twirling in shaggy drape,
leaves coarsely curled, flapping to Stravinsky,
sashaying, festooned in yippy light.

Sunflower leaf arms wound round each others' waists,
bowing forward, then raising up their seedy heads,
that show in spotlight their consuming threat,
as down the line, a silent scream escapes.

[...]

Scene iii

Now, the stage of Auvers darkens,
as if engraved with increased cross-hatch.
A thick obsidian outline
fences in the frolicking folly.

Obsession interlocked within itself.
Inflorescence, burnished bright
against the background mezzotint,
as if in mockery of his velvet rocking.

Marks on a music score, quarter rests
like black birds on the wing.
Van Gogh caught
between art and madness.
Caw music.

Scene iv

How sunflowers faced a stormy east,
how a child greeted the morning sun,
how dawn became him,
how that child bit his bread
into the shape of a gun,
what he did on that dark stage.

That child with a gun,
who taunted, then pulled the trigger
on the artist standing
in his painted field of wheat,
a man with sunflowers in his head.
The shot, a shout of denial.

Scene v

The yellow chair of wood and rush,
now on his table, turned upside down.
The single bed
with its cross-hatched coverlet, empty.
His unfinished painting leans against a wall,
a still life, blooming.

Through the yawn of the window,
sunflowers face west.
The green sky releases
a murder of crows.

Harbored: Lullaby for a Bomber

~Boston Marathon 2013, the capture by the FBI and
  Massachusetts State Police

Rinsed radishes rock like bright boats
in a bowl of water in my sunny kitchen sink
I pick up one red globe
and with my thumb on the knife blade
cut through the crisp
Pink stains my cool white flesh
Each radish slice a flat full moon
that falls like a body   into my skiff-shaped dish

While I work   the TV news replays in my head
The Special Tactical Operations Team
maneuvers their armored van in the night
toward the covered boat
stored in a family's backyard
The camera catches the cover's untied corner
the stain   the slow pink drips

The team's driver checks coordinates
on a screen   then hones-in with infrared
his poised pupils lock on white heat
Sweat forms above his eye and suddenly
he thinks of a boat moored on moonlit water
gently rocking his lover   but the image morphs
into a wake of salt and blood
He refocuses   turns the knob on the dash

and the robot's long thin arm unfolds
pivots   hovers over   like a winter branch
before it pricks then slits the plastic cover
Fussy   it tussles with the small uneven pieces
revealing the tethered ark beneath
and there you are
your sweet flesh beaded with sweat

So recently a child
your body limp   fetal   curled
like an iris round a dark aperture
Lost child   when you turn
in that boat of hurt
blood gathers red
oozes through your open cut

A pink stain on my cool white flesh

Lost child   you dream you rock safely
cocooned on a moonlit sea   carried far
beyond this hiding place   You whisper call
for your mother in her white gown   floating
like the moon far from you

Lost child   cradled
child gone mad   what have you done?

What if I'd been able to hold you   to rock you?
Could I   or any mother   have stopped you?

A pink stain on my cool white flesh

Broken bodies falling
through slowed time

Bodies shining like moons in my skiff-shaped dish
I dream I rock them   rock them easy

I reach for the shaker
Salt bursts   shatters around us
lights our sharp wounds

BASKERVILLE

The hounds of war sniff man's pungent wealth
Barking bombs echo and knock boys flat
When the heavy pit-lid unhinges from its locked fit
fangs tear rosy cheeks   dogs glut on throated death

As if lost on that moor   I am not fit
(my howling mind gripped by brutal death)
not fit to protect their precious inner wealth
Their bodies broken   blind eyes open   flat

BECAUSE THIS IS HOME

ANIMAL

Instead, walk on earth as the animal you are.
With bare feet, touch scented pine needle, lichen,
soft moist moss, move out to spiky grass.
See the slug's silver slime across cool mud.
Find an antidote for your soul's hot rash,
for the stinging nettle of human greed.
Rub red elderberry on humanity out of control
and repeat, *This is home.*

WHY STUDENTS STARE OUT THE WINDOW
—IF THERE IS ONE

this room dusty under dim light
with sharp points of fluorescent pain
a thoughtless mismatch of proportion and clutter

the predictable bite of repetition
the same talk   a buzz
one is dying to swat

this room
stuffy chalky sweaty
lacking oxygen

the surfaces here
all the same   hard and cold
stale resignation

the movement here so small
aching with constraint and stiff discomfort

::::

rather
the lush color of daybreak
the rich resonance of music

the bracing air
of mountain snow
or windy surf
the green perfume of garden

a warm breeze
the feel of newborn skin
fresh cold water

the quiet circle of choreography
the satisfaction of a body
alive with energy

chiming

House Cleaning

1

She folds the white sheets and pillowcases,
just so, and the sun-yellow towel
she used long ago
to dry and hold her small sons.

She thinks, if this gorgeous winter Solstice light
can now be so easily virtually viewed,
in the future, which kind of knowing
will be counted more true?

Will we relish our inheritance of body and its need
to praise the earth with more than naming?
Vigilant, alert, will we lightly work this beauty,
this rage for order we crave of touchable things?

Will anyone ever wish to sweep a floor
after these grandmothers fade?

2

Will anyone talk to this table whose legs,
still gnarled with tree, were turned by hand
and sing to the startled turquoise chair,
on which a barefoot child once loved to stand?

She remembers to dust the lamp,
so warm under the rose-colored shade
and places it back with care, just there, touching it
with one hand, then, why not, with the other.

[. . .]

She enjoys the quirky kick of wrapping a gift,
each wrap unique. She cleanly creases the paper corners
without a rip, and with her baby finger,
tacks down the pink ribbon about to slip,

hears the paper's crunch and ribbon's zip
as scissors pull the curl.

3

In the closet's layered shadows,
she turns her buttoned shirt fronts to her weak hand
grabs each hanger with her strong.
Only sharpened pencils are returned to the drawer.

In cupboards, coffee mugs are positioned
with handles set, like clock hands, to four.
Will human compulsion remain
to place like together with like,

light a match, hammer a nail, scour the tub?
Will it be a privilege to scrub with vinegar
on our hands and knees?
She dreams of holding

the selfish, the greedy, the brutal at bay,
and pleads to protect the trees, the trees—

4

She cares less and less for what she has not
and more for what she has, prays our Solstice light
will not be smoked and smothered.
Sunlight tastes scrumptious on her skin,

far better than sitting near its digital copy,
made now, from tiny chips, flat and laser-cracked.
With a pleasure of touch
unknown to machines, she dusts and dusts,

sings a cleaning of gutters prayer, a song
for every task, asks her sons
to love life unabashed,
asks them to hum a lullaby for home,

a human hum,
when they release her ash.

A Cordial Welcome

Chartreuse
40-69% (at least) by volume   potent
Proof (US): 80-138
Bouquet equivalent to the Monastery's 130 herbs

—a recipe that takes time and a monk's quiet hours

:::

On our walk in the forest this morning
let's give thanks
for monks   and mist not rain
and call it what you will   pungent sour mud
and for the utter softness of years and death
that pillows each step as we disturb the dew

thanks for sturdy fir trunks whose dark boughs
dangle veils of pale green
and for the silent sweet scent of bark crusted
from decades of winter's rough
and thanks for this earth scattered with
mouse-shaped cones and maple whirligigs

Let's imbibe this distillation of fir needle and
bitter herbs   this sap   that burns all the way down
the sharp taste   like a snap of twig
that keeps us alert   yet gives
a sugar high so we loosen up

Let any chattering mechanical thoughts
decay   dissolve   become detritus   as we
sip this version of velvet liqueur

We sight a line along a massive nurse log
from mossy muff to muff
under spotty clouds of ouzo mist
precipitated by this mix

of moisture and tufted licorice fern
profuse enough   to seduce

The whole kit and caboodle exudes calm
like a seasoned monk offering a balm
that tastes of Chartreuse

MORNING

Memory burns orange
through my translucent eyelids
that warm as the sun roars

Mist rises off the ridge
of the birdhouse   caresses
the maple after night's heat

Under dew's prism blanket
chartreuse moss glows
released from earth's
deep purple arms

Wet webs sparkle their magic
through my window   through the wisp of steam
that lingers here above my coffee cup

I smell music

LELOOSKA

He Who Cuts Against Wood with a Knife

His intimate tone and rhythms, his whisper words
ride the swirl of smoke rising above a crackling fire.
Resonant, they wrap us like the red and black blanket
draped over his shoulders, his chest a massive wall
set with pearl buttons, animal eyes that glint
from the edge of darkness,

Clap! like a cupboard door slam

and a masked head suddenly appears,
Raven jumps forward
with painted eye sockets like loaves of bread.
Wood strikes wood, sudden, sharp,
and Raven's face splits in half as its two doors part
revealing a second inner mask of
cedar grain that glows with fire's heat.

Then Quick! Catch it! Another break!
With eyes grown large, like Owl, like Thunderbird,
and animated by the voiceless echoes of long-ago elders,
Ancestor Spirit, now human, zooms forth, stares out.
Ovoid eyes that see within, within.

:::

Mask of Transformation,
the Past, tufted, hairy, hinged to
the iridescent Present,
the Present pivoting,
passing by before we barely taste it, birthing
the Future with its feathered questions, dark or bright.

Yet as we watch, animal eyes glint
and time disappears
Clap!   like smoke in the night.

LAUNDRY

Years of experience carrying clothes
down the stairs   then up again
The open door of the washer
like the mouth of a priest
saying the prayer of absolution
like I imagine confession
Every week as I dump the load from the full hamper
I say to myself   *But I have nothing to confess*

The washer cleans and rinses   turns through time
The dryer cycle buzzes
I gather the fresh warm clothes   relax and
sigh as I fold their new-born smell into myself
and realize   regardless of my words
that once again we have been forgiven

Ekphrastic in Anaphora

a Meditation

~after Cai Guo-Qiang's installation, *Inopportune: Stage One*, 2004

we live in the world where explosions kill people

Another car bombed
How do we hold this human horror?
Like the artist Cai Guo-Qiang   I lament   I mourn

Cai's nine nice cars defy gravity   cartwheeling over my head
nine nice cars   seen as one in stop-action   a car bombed
but here   the one last car lands *safely, undamaged, unharmed*

Nine nice cars   sprouting long tubes of blinking lights
Each car a call   a sequenced declaration
to interpret like a rune

confronting tragic truth
with a lacework of light   with beauty
however inopportune

Beauty   not just pretty
but a designed order   that implies a meaning
we seem to need

This installation keeps transforming   or do we?
The cars hold still   We're the ones moving
but we don't just escape and land free

Sometimes when it appears I'm holding still
I'm actually driving full tilt
and often   when it seems I'm going full tilt

[. . .]

instead I've slammed on the brakes   and
like these nine nice cars   I float above
hang out in the beyond

Nine nice cars   each car a charm   an incantation
enhanced with multichannel multicolored LEDs
Nine nice cars   not being destroyed   just lit up   gorgeous

:::

Beauty arrives   and shakes you   and once in it
you can see so much of the power of the universe—
how we came to be

I somersault
The lovely diffuse light behind the cars
reminds me of the slow making of art

like a laying down
of sheets on the bed…
for lovemaking

a transit through matter   slipping into and out of
appearance and erasure   the self   and other   laid bare
a space where *these grand ideas about the cosmos* are bearable

where I'm okay   even delighted
when energy flashes through nine nice cars
as perfect pulses of sequined light

like all our exquisite moments passing
Could this exchange be   a lovemaking?   I ascend
both lost and found   into these fireworks of beauty

Nine nice cars   these blinking lights looped on repeat
Can beauty   like laughter   contagious   subversive
mitigate fear and grief?

Can we just float here   suspend disbelief?
Like nine cats with nine lives
these nine nice cars are in such great shape

like us   beautiful   not yet blown apart
like us flashing   as we keep tumbling
through transformation

as we keep exploding

* italicized lines from Cai Guo-Qiang

ARCHES

Like honey in the early evening sun   the wood
studs and struts of the newly framed house
across the street glow   throw back their light

Their angled shapes remind me of the
cockeyed cathedral arches that have lined
the north section of freeway all this spring

There   among building-sized excavators
yellow bulldozers and backhoes
monumental cranes overlap their diagonal booms
of crossed and filigreed steel   forming arches
silhouetted and stark

The way at dawn   they invite in the sky
and call forth hymns from hummingbird cars
that zip by with our prayers

Notes, Inspirations & Citations

"The Blue Guitar Advances Through Time, an Ode to David Hockney"

Pablo Picasso: *The Old Guitarist*

Wallace Stevens: "The Man with the Blue Guitar"

David Hockney: *Invented Man Revealing Still Life; Self-Portrait with Blue Guitar; Tick It, Tock It, Turn It True;* and *Model with Unfinished Self-Portrait*

"A Cordial Welcome"

wikipedia.org/wiki/Chartreuse_(liqueur)

"Lelooska, *He Who Cuts Against Wood with a Knife*"

"Chief Lelooska was known as a sculptor, scholar, and educator of North American tribal traditions, particularly those of the Pacific Northwest. He directed public presentations in a Kwakwaka'wakw ceremonial house at the Lelooska Foundation and Cultural Center." (https://www.lelooska.org)

"Ekphrastic in Anaphora, a Meditation"

"Spirituality, Chaos, and *Inopportune*," Interview with Cai Guo-Qiang, (https://art21.org/read/cai-guo-qiang-spirituality-chaos-and-inopportune/)

The italicized lines in my poem are actual or slight variations of quotations from the above article.

Acknowledgments & Gratitude

"Relative" was previously published in *Verseweavers* (No. 21, 2016) and won second-place in the Oregon Poetry Association Spring Poetry Contest.

Thank you to Shawn Aveningo Sanders and Robert Sanders at The Poetry Box for accepting *Lamplight*. Their cheerful expertise during the entire publishing process has been both informative and a delight. My gratitude to Shawn for her insightful and sensitive editing.

These poems were written over many years, but all the work has been influenced by my writer friends who have encouraged me both personally, and certainly, by the example of their own fine creative efforts.

I especially wish to thank David Biespiel, Tricia Knoll, and Jules Ohman for their kind words after reading *Lamplight*. My gratitude also to Gloria Freshley, Catherine Freshley, Jennifer Dorner, and Dan Ehrenfreund who read the collection and offered valuable written comments.

And to all my dear long-time friends and family, thank you again for your love.

Early Praise

Lamplight is both opening and closing. Like any journey-woman on a quest to understand grief, Cathy Cain finds not truth so much as renewal. These poems are like compact, inescapable dreams, bruised with switchbacks that "shift / over the edge," where misery becomes a glow, a shine, and, finally, a blaze of love.

—David Biespiel, author of *Republic Café*

Cathy Cain's *Lamplight* explores what lights the darkest nights and how dark those nights can be. She writes to "wear down in poem the pointed pain." Cain, an artist (as well as poet) who works in several media, offers dramatic images to pitch opposites against each other. We find sparkling songs and savage blues, lamplight and dark. Her lyric poetry balances shadows of grief and time. Narrative poems, with touches of surrealism, explore loss, illness, and madness. She offers lights in a hospital window across a courtyard as relief. Cain plumbs the quicksand of current geo-politics. Concluding poems offer comfort in the lush color of daybreak. Her poems come home to gratitude in a morning walk, the smell of forgiveness in clean laundry. She invites the sky in at dawn.

—Tricia Knoll, author of *The Unknown Daughter*
and *Wild Apples*

Cathy Cain's poems move through lamplit rooms and find everything we've left there, everything we've hidden. The poems in *Lamplight* bring the world out of silhouette and into the lived-in body. They help us see the treachery and loveliness living within us, and show us where to go. This collection is beautifully written and powerful.

—Jules Ohman, author of *Body Grammar*

About the Author

Poet and artist **Cathy Cain** is the author of *The Weight of Clouds* (2022), *A Shape of Sky* (2021), and *Bee Dance* (2019), all from The Poetry Box press. She's additionally published a chapbook, *Empty Space Places You* (2018) from Finishing Line Press.

Cain's honors include the Edwin Markham Prize for Poetry, the Paulann Petersen Award for Poetry from Willamette Writers, and a First Place and other citations from the Oregon Poetry Association. Her poetry has appeared in *Reed Magazine, The Poeming Pigeon, Verseweavers, VoiceCatcher,* and in */pān| dé | mïk/ 2020: An Anthology of Pandemic Poems.*

Cain is a two-year Poets Studio alumna and a past Atheneum fellow, both at the Attic Institute of Arts and Letters in Portland, Oregon. She has studied with visiting poets hosted by Portland's Literary Arts and at the Mountain Writers Series. Cain holds degrees in literature and visual art from Lewis & Clark College, MAT; Oregon State University, BFA; and University of Washington, BA, Phi Beta Kappa. She has also studied at the Pacific Northwest College of Art.

Cain taught in the public schools for over thirty years. She is the lucky wife of a sweet man, and the mother of two fine sons. She lives with her husband near Portland.

About The Poetry Box®

The Poetry Box, a boutique publishing company in Portland, Oregon, provides a platform for both established and emerging poets to share their words with the world through beautiful printed books and chapbooks.

Feel free to visit the online bookstore (thePoetryBox.com), where you'll find more titles including:

The Squannacook at Dawn by Richard Jordan

Inside, Outside by Kirsten Morgan

Reading Wind by Carol Barrett

Journey of Trees by Susan Landgraf

Vitals & Other Signs of Life by David A. Goodrum

White Sail at Midnight by Ginny Lowe Connors

Chaos & Calm by Anglika Quirk

Acceleration Due to Gravity by Heikki Huotari

Life in No Ordinary Time by Laurel Feigenbaum

Field Notes from an Illusion by Lois Levinson

The Catalog of Small Contentments by Carolyn Martin

When All Else Fails by Lana Hechtman Ayers

This Is the Lightness by Rachel Barton

Self Dissection by Amelia Diaz Ettinger

Kansas Reimagined by Anara Guard

Rescue Dogs by Fred Zirm

and more . . .

Milton Keynes UK
Ingram Content Group UK Ltd.
UKHW050921231124
451587UK00021B/311

9 781956 285741